CORONA DIARY

CORONA DIARY

Pandemic Poems and Lockdown Lyrics

by

Nick Toczek

written daily

Volume 1: mid-March - end of June 2020

Copyright © 2020 Nick Toczek

Front cover: copyright © 2020 Matt Webster

First published in the United Kingdom in 2020 by
Mutiny 2000 Publications

This edition published in 2022 by
LS Arts

www.leeds-streets.uk

www.nicktoczek.com

Book layout and design by Matt Webster.

All rights reserved. No part of this publication may be reproduced, stored in a retrieval system, or transmitted, in any form or by any means, electronic, mechanical, recording or otherwise, other than for 'fair use' as brief quotations embodied in articles and reviews, without the prior permission of the publisher and copyright holder.

British Library Cataloguing in Publication Data

A catalogue record for this book is available from the British Library.

ISBN 978-1-7391481-2-6

INTRODUCTION

From mid-March 2020 I've been writing a daily poem, each documenting and reflecting an aspect of living through the coronavirus pandemic. I'm doing this partly to keep me motivated as a writer during these disturbing times and partly to create a poetic Pepysian diary of the experience.

Each evening, I've been posting the day's new poem on my Facebook page and on the Cornaverses Facebook page set up by my friend and fellow performer-poet, Janine Booth. I started doing so without expecting much response. It therefore came as a pleasant surprise when the poems began to find a steadily growing readership, with many of them being shared on other Facebook pages. Some have since been published in journals and anthologies. Others have been used as lyrics by singer-songwriters.

Now, while I continue to write and post more daily poems, here's my collection of those I wrote during the first three-and-a-half months. What you get, then, is a set of 108 poems to which I've appended a coronavirus timeline, compiled in the hope that it'll help you to more easily place my poems back within their original context.

I've no plans to stop writing. It's a beguiling process, not least because most days, as I sit down to write, I've absolutely no idea what's about to materialise. I'm already thirteen poems into Volume 2 and, remarkably, find myself still rising to the challenge. And, of course, like me, the pandemic is very far from finished.

Here, then, is Volume 1.

Nick Toczek, 14 July 2020.

ACKNOWLEDGEMENTS

We're So Safe and **Be Positive, Be Keener** have both been published in *CoronaVerses*, the anthology compiled, edited and published by Janine Booth.

Five Linked Limericks and **Unspeakable** have both been published in the anthology *The Book of Hope*, edited and published by Gary J Gill.

Dead Rite has been published in the special pandemic issue (#19) of *The Pangolin Review*.

Carehome Ghosts Speaking has been published in *Poetry's Not F***ing Boring*, the Bradford Fringe Festival 2020 poetry anthology edited by Luke Hogarth.

Conversation With The Virus is to be published in 2021 in the Shoestring Press anthology *Lockdown and After* edited by Merryn Williams.

Some Days Under Lockdown and **When Lives Don't Matter** are both to be published in *Lockdown Poetry* edited and published by Seema Gill.

About thirty of the poems have also been performed by the author in various video shows (*World Poetry Cafe*, *Poetry's Not F***ing Boring*, a *CoronaVerses* performance event, etc.) each posted on Facebook, YouTube and similar internet sites.

CONTENTS

MARCH

Covid-19 1
We're So Safe 2
Dead Rite 4
Limerick 5
Poem For A Few Weeks From Now 6
Grim As This… 7
Be Positive, Be Keener 8
Simply To Live By… 9
Back Garden 10
To Donald Trump Who's Calling It The Chinese Virus .. 11
Close Up 12
Acrostic Odes 13
Utterly Unprepared 14
How To Pass The Time While You Isolate 15
Celebrating The Joys Of This Singular Spring .. 16

APRIL

NHS Acrostic 18
Unspeakable 19
Where Are You Now, You Cocky Bastard? 20
The Dead 22
Wishes 23
Regular Handwashing 24
Only The Virus 25
This 26
Sympathising With The Tories 27
April, Cruelest Month, Brings Us… 28
Poem To Each UK MP 29
Conversation With The Virus 30

Poem For Boris Johnson 31
It's All About You 32
Because Interviewed Experts Begin Each Reply With
"So…" 33
We're All Here 34
The Virus Addresses The World 35
Stalker 36
The Two Of Us 37
Unfaithful 38
Via Us 39
Game #1 40
Game #2 41
Shall 42
8 Pm Every Thursday 43
Separation 44
At The End Of Lockdown 45
Corona Blues 46
The Cost 48
A Testing Time… At Last! 49

MAY

Come What May 50
Poem For Matt Hancock, Health Secretary 51
Second Peak 52
Your Life Under Lockdown 53
Carers 54
Almost Forty Thousand Dead Here In Britain Alone 55
Clapping Verses 56
Oh, A Nature Poem! 57
Of Course We Miss… 58
Lessons 59
They Make No Sense 60
Mixed Messages 61

Landscapes By Hieronymus Bosch 62
Tell Johnson And Trump We're Not At War 63
Short Sentences 64
Five Linked Limericks 65
Because Of Our Impatience 66
Reopening Schools The Week After Next? 68
A Week Of Gardening During Lockdown 69
While I'm Out Walking With My Bloody Mutt 70
Wish List 71
Normal 72
Doubters' Creed 73
A Poem About You, Dominic Cummings 74
Carehome Ghosts Speaking 75
Press Conference 76
Johnson's Latest Baby 77
Anticipation 78
We 79
Poem For My Partner 81
Tory Bastards In September / October 82

JUNE

Ending The Honeymoon 83
Imagined Guest 84
Signing Out 85
Surrounded By Idiots 86
We Poets, Adverbally 87
If I Were The Virus 88
Government Will Duck The Blame 90
For Those Who Still Trust Our Governing Gang 91
Where I Went During Lockdown 92
As We Hit More Than Sixty Thousand 'Excess' Deaths .. 94
Loner 96
We've Been Shopped 97

Some Days Under Lockdown 98
Evening Walk 99
The Virus Invites You…..100
We Weren't Always Old 101
Their New 'World-Class' Track'n'trace Phone App 102
Just A List… 103
Run By The Bullingdon Boys 105
Life Will Be Better When… 106
When Lives Don't Matter 107
Two Metres Down To One 108
If This Virus Kills Me, Here's What I Did Well...............109
The Rag Trade Reopens 110
Marooned 111
Why Reopen Everything?...112
When This Virus Hits Its Second Spike...........................113
Sea Fever 114
Sea Fever 115
Covid-19'S Leicester Press Conference 116
Build Build Build 117

COVID-19

The first UK covid death was in early March.

Okay, we're mortal, but pause to admire us.
Like our computers we're fighting our virus,
Won't let it scare us, defeat us or tire us.

Respiratory rather than renal or thyrous,
It's proving fatal. That's hardly desirous.
Tell the Grim Reaper he doesn't require us.

Tell our employers they don't need to fire us.
World goes to shit, we'll go back to papyrus.
Talk to survival and tell it to hire us.

WE'RE SO SAFE

Government spokespersons tried to quell panic with their 'Stay Safe' slogan. My spellcheck kept correcting 'covid' to 'corvid' which is a crow. Appropriately, the collective noun for crows is a murder. One of my favourite Facebook posts was a picture of two crows subtitled 'attempted murder'.

Safe as where what's ghostly goes is
Safe as ghastly when it grows is
Safe as plague and ring of roses

Safe as fighting off your foes is
Safe as fright as figures froze is
Safe as hopelessness proposes

Safe as sentenced to death-rows is
Safe as murdering of crows is
Safe as daily news discloses

Safe as touching lip or nose is
Safe as wash your hands of those is
Safe as when their coffin closes

Safe as poetry and prose is
Safe as fast which never slows is
Safe as when your driver dozes

Safe as world and all its woes is
Safe as faith which never shows is
Safe as tablets can't cure Moses

Safe as ventilator hose is
Safe as all that no one knows is
Safe as every question poses

Safe as how this wild wind blows is
Safe as where our future flows is
Safe as contact risk exposes.

Stay safe…
Safe till virus metamorphoses.

DEAD RITE

The daily news had become a relentlessly escalating numbers game.

Dead right that we're globally under attack.
This world we've been trashing is trashing us back.
We took it for granted. We're watching it crack.

Though lifelong we've always been part of the pack
Our self-isolation sees us on our jack.
We've no one. We've nothing to take a new tack.

We're losing the pattern, the plot and the track.
Our families and neighbours lie stretched on this rack.
We're sick and it sucks cos they'll give us the sack.

This tightrope we're walking seems suddenly slack.
Where there's no known cure for these coughs we can't
                                                hack
We've some who won't make it. We've those we'll soon
                                                lack.

Like junkies grown drunken on skunk, coke and smack
Our interest is fading. Our daylight grows black.
We're restless. We clock-watch. We're insomniac.

We're groping for answers. While facing fresh flak
We swim through statistics. The numbers don't stack.
Grim Reaper's here mouthing: 'hypochondriac'.

LIMERICK

I've lived with prostate cancer for 2 years. One squatter's enough.

The virus we're calling Corona
Which squats in the lungs of each owner
Pays nothing in rent
Just stays till they're spent
This sly 20-20 death-donor.

POEM FOR A FEW WEEKS FROM NOW

I'm married to a senior manager in the NHS. They were preparing for the worst.

A silence like dumb desperation
Or some slightly numb dislocation
Treads every dread street of this nation.

You think this a strange situation.
No people. Are they on vacation?
Or moved to another location?

You're puzzled. Why such consternation?
It's simple. There's one explanation
For this abrupt depopulation.

Ignoring the viral gestation
We mingled for food and libation,
For travel, work and recreation.

We thus met with annihilation,
Our lungs all deprived of aeration.
Survivors hide in isolation.

GRIM AS THIS…

Even the ordinary and everyday had become threatening.

Grim as this fear when we're simply out shopping.
Grim as hand-washing and wiping and mopping.
Grim as news stories we're posting and swapping.

Grim as health services all belly-flopping.
Grim as each labouring lung stalling, stopping.
Grim as these losses like limbs that we're lopping.

Grim as this daily death-toll that's not dropping.
Grim as the count goes from small up to whopping.
Grim as the long list this virus is cropping.

BE POSITIVE, BE KEENER

After half a dozen dark poems, I needed to write something brighter.

Fewer planes are flying now.
This planet's getting greener.
Fewer cars are on the roads.
The air is getting cleaner.

Pubs are shut. We're drinking less.
Already we've grown leaner
On water, coffee, cocoa,
Tea, orange juice, Ribena.

At least we're trapped in this place,
Not Halifax or Heanor.
We're nicer to each other
In everyday demeanour.

Way things are, we wash a lot
Which makes us much hygiener.
And we're both stuck at home where
We two can get obscener.

SIMPLY TO LIVE BY...

When I posted this on Facebook, many people shared it.

Save a neighbour, sister, brother,
Friend or worker, father, mother.
Not to gather.
Not together.
Stay away from one another.

BACK GARDEN

*Lockdown entailed learning to do
as we were told.*

Evenings and mornings,
in this water-thin
slanting Spring sunlight,
midges mass and mingle.

We don't. We stay single.
We heed our hard warnings.

These nights grow cold.
We wake to frost and
lost at home at first
we stall but soon re-start.

We keep ourselves apart.
We do as we've been told.

We mow, trim borders,
plant seed and feed the birds,
hang out washing,
do more garden chores.

We then return indoors.
We obey their orders.

TO DONALD TRUMP WHO'S CALLING IT THE CHINESE VIRUS

This was near the beginning of the U.S. president's unfathomable denial of the obvious threat.

It's not where it comes from,
It's where the thing's going.
You point your short finger
Without even knowing.

It's when numbers dying
Will start to cease growing.
You shrug off these losses
To keep finance flowing.

It's what can be done to
Get this virus slowing.
You feather your nest while
You're tweeting and crowing.

It's all of those deaths that
Your policy's sowing.
You're deaf, dumb and blind to
This dead wind that's blowing.

It's counting the countless
Whose lives you are throwing.
You don't see the dying,
Just profit beats owing.

CLOSE UP

*I wanted to write a poem which stood beside
the beds of the sick and the dying.*

Inhale, exhale; inhale, exhale.
Listen to lungs. Don't let them fail.
Weak where once they blew a gale.
Hear them whistle. How they wail.

Inhale, exhale; inhale, exhale.
These ribs are bars which built this jail.
Each breath an inmate begging bail.
There's no reprieve. No call. No mail.

Inhale, exhale; inhale, exhale.
Never known struggling on this scale.
Failure at the speed of a snail.
And, oh, it leaves a dreadful trail.

Inhale, exhale; inhale, exhale.
It's crucifixion, nail by nail.
A sacrifice beyond the pale.
A landed fish to flap, to flail.

Inhale, exhale; inhale, exhale.
One day this wind will fill our sail.
One day we'll live to tell this tale.
One day our souls won't be for sale.

ACROSTIC ODES

I've always hated acrostics. This was the first I'd ever written.

Only ask where this all heads:
Dearth of doctors, too few beds,
Everyone deprived of meds.

Optimism's slashed to shreds.
Day by day this virus spreads
Emptying each trail it treads.

Outcomes every witness dreads
Dangle lives from slender threads,
Endings blunt as pencil leads.

UTTERLY UNPREPARED

With our government incoherent and incompetent, we felt alone.

We've empty schools and clubs and malls
And pools and pubs and concert halls.

And housebound here within four walls
We hope this virus never calls.

Our headlines clock its latest hauls
With counts of lives it stops and stalls.

We wear what stuff we're told forestalls:
Masks, hats and visors, scarves and shawls.

None can foresee what next befalls
Our own and others' urban sprawls.

Invisible, unheard, it crawls
From lung to lung. This toll appalls.

We wish it came with caterwauls,
With yelps and yells and yowls and yawls.

We'd all fight back. We've got the balls.
But we're without the wherewithals.

HOW TO PASS THE TIME WHILE YOU ISOLATE

Lockdown became dull and repetitive, a tunnel with no visible end.

Walk from your front door to your garden gate.
Talk to yourself. Try to have a debate.

Scroll your way through Facebook for eight hours
straight.
Patrol the whole of Netflix, dusk till late.

Make a meagre meal. Maybe masturbate.
Take a ton of selfies. Infatuate.

Beware of you because you're not your mate.
Declare your home an autonomous state.

Winge to your friends down the phone about fate.
Binge the bloody news till your eyes dilate.

Shop on eBay. Buy some crap that looks great.
Stop by your letterbox and wait and wait.

Lag, linger, loiter, loll, procrastinate,
Drag, defer, delay and then vacillate.

Now the same again and then duplicate
How you pass the time while you isolate.

CELEBRATING THE JOYS OF THIS SINGULAR SPRING

A sofa catalogue posted through our letterbox from DFS was crassly headed: 'The Joys Of Spring!'

Jump and jive! Jump and jive!

You and I've
been cut loose from the human hive.
You and I've
no bus to catch, no rush-hour drive.
You and I've
got weeks without our nine-to-five.

Jump and jive! Jump and jive!

You and I've
not got pissed in a nearby dive.
You and I've
no work excuses to contrive.
You and I've
no cause to lie, we're free to skive.

Jump and jive! Jump and jive!

You and I've
now nowhere urgent to arrive.
You and I've
no low co-workers who connive.
You and I've
no management to make us strive.

Jump and jive! Jump and jive!

You and I've
gained time to spare and time to thrive.
You and I've
got every reason to survive.
You and I've
to celebrate that we're alive.

So jump and jive! Jump and jive!
Just
  jump
    and
      jive!

NHS ACROSTIC

The underfunded NHS was struggling to cope.

Now
Here's
Something…

No
Help
Since
Nineteen…
Hmm…
Sixties?

Neglectful
Handouts
Sufficed.
Nurses
Hardly
Salaried.

Negative
Hospital
Support.
Numbers
Hired
Squeezed.

Nearly
Half
Staff
Necessary
Have
Scarpered.

Now
Hundreds
Suffocate.
Nobody
Has
Solutions.

Nothing
Happens.
Still
None
Harbour
Shame.

Not
Hierarchy,
Say
Nation's
Hopeless
Statesmen.

UNSPEAKABLE

Responding lamentably to our soaring death-toll, the government blatantly lied.

There is no truth.
There are no facts.
Just lies to hide the blame.

Press questions ducked
By spokespersons,
Their waffle limply lame.

Try asking why
So many die.
They'll simply say the same:

Community
Immunity
And death's a numbers game.

Procrastinate
Then act too late.
It's wise to wait, they claim.

They got it wrong
Did all along
And still they show no shame.

WHERE ARE YOU NOW, YOU COCKY BASTARD?

As part of the complacent society which elected this government, we weren't blameless.

We were once so confident.
We used to be so sure
About where we were going
But we're not anymore.

We'd visions of tomorrow
Had faith in what we saw
With hopes and plans and places
We'd visit and explore.

And then came this pandemic
For which there's no known cure
This dragon come among us
This unseen carnivore.

We were the western wealthy
Who grew up wanting more
And relished self-indulgence
And thought we knew the score.

But then this beast descended
Like life's dark fatal flaw.
We thought we'd seen everything.
We've not seen this before.

We've cancelled aspirations
Deleted dates galore
And, now in isolation,
We hear the dragon's roar.

So here we are in hiding
And who knows what's in store?
We're losing every battle
Led unarmed into war.

THE DEAD

Four days after I wrote this, the virus killed John Prine, one of my favourite songwriters.

We've journalists listing the numbers who go.
Their increase initially seems safely slow.
So, caution and concern remain fairly low,
With crowds filling tube trains, each school, pub and
                                                              show.

When this weather changes, much colder winds blow.
The 'yes we can mingle' soon alters to 'no'
And feathers of fear flutter, black as their crow
While daily we witness what rate these deaths grow.

Dear God, we're now losing the people we know.
We're all heirs to shares in Pandemic and Co.
We're seeds which this virus has chosen to sow.
We're crops in the fields that its grim reapers mow.

WISHES

We all need a wish-list.

I wish we all were less afraid.
I wish away these rules obeyed.
I wish this virus had decayed.
I wish no lungs let it invade.

I wish for life like lemonade.

I wish our colours had not greyed.
I wish attention had been paid.
I wish mistakes had not been made.
I wish for days less retrograde.

I wish for crowd and loud parade.

I wish this nightmare would now fade.
I wish it gone, not just delayed.
I wish to blunt its bitter blade.
I wish to wash away its trade.

I wish for where we've holidayed.

I wish no grave, no priest, no spade.
I wish the ferryman unpaid.
I wish a cure, not this tirade.
I wish my messages relayed.

I wish not mask, but masquerade.

REGULAR HANDWASHING

This became a ritual for us all.

I stir. I wake. I wash my hands.
I snooze. Daybreak. I wash my hands.
I've food to make. I wash my hands.
I fry. I bake. I wash my hands.

I grill a steak. I wash my hands.
I eat pancake. I wash my hands.
A thirst to slake. I wash my hands.
I drink milkshake. I wash my hands.

I shop. Queues snake. I wash my hands.
We crowd. I quake. I wash my hands.
A friend. Handshake. I wash my hands.
That's my mistake. I wash my hands.

I need a break. I wash my hands.
A walk to take. I wash my hands.
The park. The lake. I wash my hands.
Feed duck and drake. I wash my hands.

Skin starts to flake. I wash my hands.
With life at stake, I wash my hands.
Come cough, headache. I wash my hands.
For heaven's sake. I wash my hands.

ONLY THE VIRUS

Global travel had stopped. Only the virus travelled freely.

Our planes are down. We've empty air.
And we're not going anywhere.
We're home and held by rare despair
With our own company to bear.

Only the virus doesn't care.
The world's become its thoroughfare.
It can and does go everywhere,
No passport and it pays no fare.

So, where's it bound? We're unaware.
It could come here. It could go there.
Wherever it goes, we'd best beware
Lest our own lungs become its lair.

Only the virus sets this snare,
Broadcasting its disrepair.
A nomad with one gift to share,
This plague to which we're all laid bare.

Corona's grossly grown affair:
From Finisterre to Delaware,
Bonaire to Weston-super-Mare,
We've millions needing Medicare.

Only the virus roves elsewhere,
Enters bodies it'll impair,
Steals breath and then injects nightmare.
Sheer chance selects which ones to spare.

THIS

The beast was among us.

This is the monster, the mythical worm.
This is more thick-skinned than your pachyderm.
This is the virus much worse than a germ.

This is not here for a limited term.
This is the permanent wave become perm.
This is where birth and death meet in the sperm.

This is the stuff that makes innocence squirm.
This is what picks on the old and infirm.
This the pandemic which corpses confirm.

SYMPATHISING WITH THE TORIES

In a Northern accent, so 'staff' & 'scarf' don't rhyme.

Running this country has gotta be naff.
Apes await wise words from you, their giraffe.
How do you – public schooled – talk to riffraff?
They grunt. You warble like finch or chiffchaff.

Running this country has gotta be naff.
Now, with this virus, it's double the faff,
MPs and bosses and government staff
Having to come up with graph after graph.

Running this country has gotta be naff,
Shutting down library, pub, shop and caff,
Getting the plebs to all stay in their gaff,
Calling in squaddies, the navy, the raf.

Running this country has gotta be naff,
Your leisurely life left less than a laugh:
Empty decanter and empty carafe.
Pity you, thirsty, with nothing to quaff.

APRIL, CRUELEST MONTH, BRINGS US...

More about life under lockdown. It was T.S. Eliot who called April the cruelest month.

Nothing much that's satisfying.

TV programmes magnifying
What's already petrifying.
Politicians justifying,
Just avoiding specifying.
Petty pundits prophesying.
World so weird we're wonder why-ing.

We wade through the falsifying.
Loonies flood the web with lying.
Rumours spread that fools are buying.
None of this is edifying.
Nutters on-line all denying
Meds and beds, the dead, the dying.

Airports empty. No planes plying.
Only birds and insects flying.
Like our hands, we're washed-out, drying.
Locked down, parted, not nearby-ing.
We should all be out there lying
On our hotel sunbeds frying.

Instead, inside, in bed, sighing,
Lost and listless, hardly trying,
Sometimes angry, sometimes crying,
Mostly merely mummifying
Home's this hole we're occupying.
Oh, it's dull, this death-defying.

POEM TO EACH UK MP

UK MPs awarded themselves grants of up to
£10,000 for working at home and the same again
for closing their offices.

Blow you and your bloody blether
Claiming we're in this together
Like you care one fig or feather.
You can shove it up your nether.

Like a dog pulls on its tether
You bank big bucks, hell-for-leather.
Foodbank queues? You mouth "Whatever",
Were you ever bothered? Never.

Virus rages. Lifelines sever
Yet you spot a good endeavour.
Frontline workers die… however
Shares are cheap. Investing's clever.

This your free world. This its weather.
Kill the poor. Stay rich forever.

CONVERSATION WITH THE VIRUS

A poem without rhyming!

'So, you're seventy this September, huh?'
'Yeah, but I look and feel younger.'
'And you've prostate cancer?'
'Low level, mate, and currently inactive.'
'And asthma?'
'Not used my inhaler for three years.'
'How come?'
'I'm a full-on fitness freak, Fitbit devotee
And daily disciple of my cross-trainer.'
'You should kick that lot into touch
And act your bloody age, my friend.'
'Why, so you can add me to your death list?'
No reply. The virus merely smiles.

POEM FOR BORIS JOHNSON

Our PM recovered from the virus and feigned full support for the NHS.

You were always all vainglory.
Nurses' pay freeze. That was Tory.
Now we hear a change of story.
Oh, hypocrisy's so hoary.

All your lies and your outlawry.
We've no call for polls by MORI.
We've no need of judge and jury.
We know underfunding's gory.

Don't pretend it's hunky-dory.
You're behind this whole furore.
Blame's – like Grenfell – multi-storey.
Endless death comes stripped of glory.

IT'S ALL ABOUT YOU

While most of us observed precautions, some didn't.

You

Kick up a fuss while stood in queues
When asked to distance, you refuse

You

Gather in gangs, not threes or twos
With park and beach as rendezvous

You

Incite your friends to break taboos
Invite them all to barbecues

You

Join party crowds for sex, drugs, booze
All human life is yours to use

You

Behave exactly as you choose
Absolutely nothing to lose…

…but you and you and you and yous
and loads and loads and loads of yous…

BECAUSE INTERVIEWED EXPERTS BEGIN EACH REPLY WITH "SO..."

This affectation is even more irritating than teen-speak which drops 'like' into every sentence.

So to the west from the east
So comes Covid, this new beast

So this virus starts to feast
So we tot up our deceased

So we vacate beach, bar, piste
So like herds of wildebeest

So in four walls, mortgaged, leased
So we lockdown unreleased

So to Trump, our arriviste
So mad, wigged-out and hair-pieced

So he's despot and high-priest
So democracy has ceased

So pandemic's top artiste
So wants money masterpieced

So blames death for gains decreased
So more die, each corpse policed

So the poor get snuffed and fleeced
So cash flows and palms get greased

So the rich see wealth increased
So not much has changed, at least.

WE'RE ALL HERE

When death came, we were baffled by it.

Worldwide, what quite brought us to this?
Alone with death, we dread its kiss.
That snake is near. We hear its hiss.

With virus cast as nemesis,
We grope for its antithesis,
Our S.O.S. as emphasis.

What did we do? What did we miss?
We yearn to learn the genesis,
The means, the metamorphosis.

Whatever the hypothesis,
When 'Why?' defies diagnosis
It frees disease to take the piss.
.
We've governments we rightly dis
And say, one day, they'll face justice
If just for their paralysis.

No cure. No hint of synthesis.
No hope. We're here, wrong side of bliss,
Left with this deft analysis:

To die's today's slow psychosis.

THE VIRUS ADDRESSES THE WORLD

We were all vulnerable.

As a virus, I'm a scary 'un
Yet I'm egalitarian

I kill

Both aesthete and barbarian
Illiterate and librarian
Anarchist and Aryan

Pop-fan and Wagnerian
Trappist and vulgarian
Huntsman and vegetarian

Leo and Saggitarian
Landowner and agrarian
Liberal and sectarian

Haitian and Hungarian
Bantu and Bulgarian
Bolivian and Bavarian

Prole and parliamentarian
Sikh and Rastafarian
Newborn and nonagenarian

Voter and totalitarian
Virgoan and Aquarian
Shaven-headed and hairy 'un.

STALKER

There was this sense of the virus being everywhere.

We've locked our doors. Yet we're on edge.
He hangs beyond our garden hedge.

He lurks in lungs. His offspring fledge
In neighbours: Ronald, Rita, Reg.

He's on their breath, their prayers, their pledge,
On supermarket meat and veg.

He haunts each handle, rail and ledge
And every nook in which to wedge.

He hovers here at whisper's edge,
In newsroom rumour, sludge and sedge.

He owns those depths these death-tolls dredge,
Has come to stay till we next sledge…

… or slay us all, so some allege.

THE TWO OF US

More about me, Gaynor, and the rigours of our lockdown.

They broadcast brews made with mirrors and smokery
Conflicting news robed in jiggery-pokery.

We swill and we swab. We're handwashing hopefully
Microbes of Covid swept down the drain soapily.

Jailed in our own joints by this deadly jokery
We're here on lockdown, held lonesomely locally.

Clapping on Thursdays is all we're left socially
Rest of the time it's just you and me, bothily.

Spending days gardening, daisily, rosily
Planting and watering, seedily, hosily.

Food from the veg man or tinned or kept frozily
Five o'clock stroll takes us round the block moseyly.

Keeping an eye on the neighbourhood nosily
Nothing much better to do I supposily.

Music on Facebook that's mostly played folkily
Little that's great but some played oky-dokily.

Late-night TV. We watch boozily, dozily
Baked couch-potatoes, we're snuggled up cosily.

UNFAITHFUL

God-bashers die like the rest of us.

In our world we've always had plagues and diseases
And now come these dry coughs, these fevers, death's
                                                          wheezes.

We thought this was flu-like, but no. No one sneezes.
It seizes the lungs and then squeezes and squeezes.

Watch worsening symptoms which nothing much eases.
No miracles these days. No cure through Lord Jesus.

But still all you faithful, will pray till Hell freezes,
Whole holes in your holiness plain as in cheeses.

It's not due to sin and some God this displeases.
Your devil's descended. Death's breath's like Spring
                                                          breezes.

VIA US

A poem which appears to be about Covid-19.

Covid-19 wholly owns us
Covid-19 clamps and cones us
Covid-19 just Jack Jones us
Covid-19 sticks and stones us
Covid-19 hunts, haunts, hones us
Covid-19 would bare bones us.

Covid-19 chaperons us
Covid-19 grants and loans us
Covid-19 tracks and drones us
Covid-19 texts and phones us
Covid-19 next de-thrones us
Covid-19 Al Capones us.

Covid-19 all alones us
Covid-19 soon postpones us
Covid-19 unknown zones us
Covid-19 moans and groans us
Covid-19 now disowns us
Covid-19 thus gravestones us.

GAME #1

No sport, so I thought of commentating on the virus.

I've heard commentators say:
'Every microbe has its day.'
'Watch the way these beggars play.'
'None of them gives much away.'

I've heard commentators say:
'Fingers crossed. We'll be okay.'
'This ain't cricket or croquet.'
'Gamesmanship has gone astray.'

I've heard commentators say:
'Seems our team's in disarray.'
'No attack. Too much delay.'
'Trust me, there'll be hell to pay.'

I've heard commentators say:
'March was bad, but April, May...'
'Tactics shot. Now they hold sway.'
'God, it's brutal, this affray.'

GAME #2

And here's the other meaning of the word game.

Corona, the hunter, now knows no shame.
He sees all human life as game.
We're merely sport, to murder, maim.
Wildlife bites back. We don't. We're tame.

Corona, the hunter, accepts no blame.
He stalks our aging, wounded, lame.
We see him pause, raise weapon, aim,
Cos every kill is his to claim.

Corona, the hunter, sits centre-frame.
We trophies amplify his fame.
So sod our family, job or name.
Just count each corpse. We're all the same.

SHALL

Short and positive at the end of a lousy night.

Shall unseat it.
Shall anon.
Shall defeat it.
Shall be gone.
Shall delete it.
Shall have shone.
Shall live sweeter.
Shall move on.

Shall sing Covid's loud swan song.

8 PM EVERY THURSDAY

*We stood outside our homes and clapped weekly
but never weakly for the NHS.*

On our street where dogs are crapping
On our street where we're back-slapping
On our street you'll find us yapping
On our street that Google's mapping
On our street we're loudly clapping.

On our street where we're rat-trapping
On our street we're overlapping
On our street with tempers snapping
On our street we've neighbours scrapping
On our street we're proudly clapping.

On our street with pigeons flapping
On our street though strength is sapping
On our street we're not caught napping
On our street where we stand rapping
On our rowdy street we're clapping.

SEPARATION

The loneliness of long-distanced lockdown.

On TV an MP says, 'stay home', then smiles.
This house-arrest holds us apart like exiles.

Out walking, two metres feels more like ten miles.
Masked, we slip swiftly down supermarket aisles.

Corona comes calling, dons guises and guiles,
Strides unseen between us with weasel-like wiles.

This, predator deadly as Nile crocodiles,
Dines out on our flesh, freedom, faith and lifestyles.

We've treasured lives measured through airpipes and dials,
Each nameless death graphed through facts, figures and
                                                            files.

These mass-executions occur without trials.
Acceptance breeds lethargy. Restlessness riles.

We cling to our floors and our walls and roof tiles,
This stockade in which we've amassed our stockpiles.

AT THE END OF LOCKDOWN

*When you're smothered in government
lies, realism matters.*

At the end of lockdown
There will be no
Lucky pots of gold for us,
Fortunes to unfold for us,
Fantasy freehold for us,
Joys in growing old for us,
Exits from this cold for us.

At the end of lockdown
There will be no
Justice to uphold to us,
Prisoners paroled to us,
Easy answers bowled to us,
Magic money dolled to us,
Satisfaction sold to us.

At the end of lockdown
There will be no
Truth to be extolled by us,
Paradise patrolled by us,
Tales of wonder told by us,
Better days enrolled by us,
New world now controlled by us.

CORONA BLUES

*For long-dead bluesman Robert Johnson
and, yeah, black lives matter.*

Standing at the crossroads
Some place I'd never been,
Met up with the devil
Dressed as a death machine,
Kind of a Corona
Known as Covid-19.

"Easy meat" he called me.
"What's that supposed mean?"
"That ya not got testin'
And need a new vaccine
Cos there ain't no genie
To save the human gene."

All the while we stood there
As minutes blew between,
He fell strangely silent,
His eyes and ears keen,
Focused on my breathing,
My lungs, my heart, my spleen.

Conversation over,
I gladly quit that scene,
Pedal flat to the floor
Back in my limousine,
Praying that plain distance
Would somehow intervene.

Fate, though, blurred the future,
Mud fogging my windscreen.
Nothing's ever easy
And some's just plain obscene:
Bodies being counted
Wrapped up in polythene.

Some days there's no washing
Will make your hands come clean.
Some encounters darken
Like cave-mouth or ravine.
Dealing with the dying
By upping their morphine.

THE COST

Mental and physical health also matter.

On lockdown, we live with psychosis
Each home-schooled on just what morose is.

News enters, as if by osmosis
And, with it, comes our new neurosis.

This latter-day tuberculosis
Corona delivered in doses.

We're taught to now know what too close is
While learning exactly what gross is.

The cost's not the dire diagnosis
The true price lies in its prognosis.

A TESTING TIME… AT LAST!

Finally our government, three murderous months too late, opted for testing.

A lifetime of self-interest… test… test… test…
Till Boris felt his lungs congest… test… test… test…
Let's hope the clown abandons jest… test… test… test…
Since he too has been NHSed… test… test… test…
Now four months late, but for the best… test… test…
                                                                         test…
Here comes some action. Who'd have guessed? … test…
                                                                          test… test…

Though not enough, it must be stressed… test… test…
                                                                          test…
Our wave of deaths is near its crest… test… test… test…
But let me get this off my chest… test… test… test…
This leadership with which we're blessed… test… test…
                                                                          test…
Cut the staff and didn't invest… test… test… test…
And voted nurses' pay suppressed… test… test… test…

Some sense, it seems, has built a nest… test… test… test…
Our frontline staff, long under-dressed… test… test…
                                                                          test…
Are being granted their request… test… test… test…
For PPE they'd not accessed… test… test… test…
The obvious at last addressed… test… test… test…
We're playing catch-up with the rest… test… test… test…

COME WHAT MAY

*A new month and a nod to Johnson's predecessor,
Theresa May.*

Living day-to-day. Virus here to stay.
Knowing we're its prey. Pray we'll be okay.
We'll die but I say let's delay the day.
So, statement, not a question: Come what May?

After life no afterlife: flesh then clay
Suddenly's easy. Slow's a lousy way.
Sod long lonely death stuck in some sickbay.
Awful April's ending so come what May?

POEM FOR MATT HANCOCK, HEALTH SECRETARY

Of all Johnson's lying toady crew, this man was perhaps the least honest.

Fiddle facts and figures, Matt,
Furthering this farce.
Pull your sound-bite triggers, Matt,
Covering your arse.

Twiddle with perceptions, Matt.
Twist the recent past.
Riddled with deceptions, Matt,
Truly you're a blast.

But truth can't be disguised, Matt,
Dismissed or denied.
No testing? Ill-advised, Matt.
That's why thousands died.

Duck another question, Matt,
Mentioning the dead.
Just a small suggestion, Matt,
Admit you were misled.

SECOND PEAK

Almost sixty years ago Bob Dylan wrote: 'It doesn't take a weatherman to know which way the wind blows'.

In our empty cafes, pubs and clubs and schools
Covid waits, smiles and says: 'Come back in, you fools.'
We'll repay his patience. We'll relax the rules.
We'll reopen markets, libraries and pools.
Covid will multiply deaths and ghosts and ghouls.

Throughout vacant venues, airports, hotels, parks
Covid prowls with tiger-claws and teeth like sharks.
'Soon they'll return to me,' he slyly remarks,
And his thin voice crackles like electric arcs.
Out there in the darkness, a startled dog barks.

In our empty restaurants, offices, shops,
In take-aways, trains and planes, and at bus stops,
Covid hides out of reach of bleach, soap and mops,
Needn't speak, knows we're weak, sees how our guard drops.
Lockdown'll loosen. He'll harvest human crops.

YOUR LIFE UNDER LOCKDOWN

More on the ups and downs of isolating.

You lose track of day and date
Do booze till you put on weight.

You snooze way past half past eight
View news, clocking each death-rate.

You cruise and procrastinate
Blue shoes, Elvis, music's great.

You choose dishes to create
Do queues shopping: wait, wait, wait.

You bruise beaten by your mate
Knew dues paid just devastate.

You, whose future falls to fate
Brew views blaming those you hate.

CARERS

I love the simple rhythms found in rhyme and repetition.

Why care that life's grown hard to bear?
Why care you're rooted to your chair?
Why care that this just drives you spare?
Why care Corona's everywhere?
Why care you're scared to breathe the air?
Why care if you've not got a prayer?
Why care? Why care? Why care?

Why care about your body hair?
Why care about the clothes you wear?
Why care your home's in disrepair?
Why care you hardly leave your lair?
Why care you only curse and swear?
Why care that this seems so unfair?
Why care? Why care? Why care?

Why care when caring's really rare?
Why care the game is solitaire?
Why care that nothing's yours to share?
Why care that you're in deep despair?
Why care when you know no one's there?
Why care about this whole nightmare?
Why care? Why care? Why care?

ALMOST FORTY THOUSAND DEAD HERE IN BRITAIN ALONE

While the government claimed some fifteen thousand fewer deaths, the Office of National Statistics gave us the staggering truth. However, people still selfishly complained.

We hear your voice whining, you winger, you moaner.
You say that you're pig-sick of being a loner.

Each radio station's self-pitying phoner
Is there to chuck bricks like some biblical stoner.

You've premises shut for six weeks. You're the owner.
You're not making money, you selfish brain-donor.

They've graves in Milan and more in Barcelona.
They've corpses from New York to south Arizona.

These dead, though, don't matter to you, our new Jonah,
Soon joined by each grunter and griper and groaner.

Pure profit paves pathways for each no-go zoner
To open for business and re-spread Corona.

CLAPPING VERSES

Thursday evening's on-street one-minute's clapping seemed insufficient.

Clap for doctors, carers, nurses.
Clap though more loss intersperses.
Clap the coffins and the hearses.

Clap when rising death reverses.
Clap those who survive these curses.
Clap more funds from public purses.

Clap the cures each lab rehearses.
Clap for safer universes.
Clap when Covid's threat disperses.

OH, A NATURE POEM!

Sitting down, usually in the evening, to write these daily poems, I'd often not know what would come. This one was a pleasant surprise.

Oh, but aren't our western politicians smooth and smug?
Oh, the slimy trail that's left by every single slug.
Oh, but soon we'll all be fine. Just trust them. Touch and
                                                                             hug.
Oh, this spring is splendid. Sit and sun yourself, you mug.

Oh, I wish when asked of deaths they wouldn't merely
                                                                           shrug.
Oh, how deep the hole that those burrowing beasts have
                                                                            dug.
Oh, we're all in this together. Feel your heartstrings tug.
Oh, how hard it is to fend off every biting bug.

Oh, but what is nature when it's money that's the drug?
Oh, but here we are at home. We're comfy, warm and
                                                                            snug.
Oh, what virus? Birdsongs choir us. We're all in a fug.
Oh, the leaves on plants and trees! The view's a bright
                                                                       green rug.

OF COURSE WE MISS…

A few of these were actually fun to write… such as this one.

Of course we miss…

Summer beaches
Handshake reaches
Sharing peaches
What life teaches
But not…
Terrorist threats
Mosquito nets
Paying our debts
Public toilets.

Of course we miss…

Outdoor events
Sensual scents
Festival tents
Foreign accents
But not…
Shave underarm
Anti-Islam
Simper and smarm
Morning alarm.

Of course we miss…

Nights in the pub
Working Men's Club
Curry-house grub
Reggae 'n' dub
But not…
Appointments missed
Things-to-do list
All alone pissed
And the dentist.

Of course we miss…

Good hotel staff
Having a laugh
Food from a caf
Jokes that are naff
But not…
Motorway queues
More Brexit news
The wrong tattoos
Shit on our shoes.

LESSONS

Here's a spooky one. I like its noir filmic quality.

I'm leaving my lockdown retreat.
It's night. You hear my pounding feet.
They beat on tarmac, flags, concrete.
I stride, repeat. I stride, repeat…

Somehow me and the microbe meet
Up on the corner of our street.
We step back, distance, nod and greet,
Use guarded words. We're both discrete.

His monotone pours clipped and neat
To ring like rain on metal sheet.
I think of butchery and meat,
A restaurant which serves defeat.

We've Covid entering to eat.
The chef is turning up the heat.
But nothing lessens. Take a seat.
We live through days left incomplete.

Think language ladled sickly-sweet
And thickly larded with deceit.
We've deaths as dense as winter sleet.
Our virus picks up the receipt.

THEY MAKE NO SENSE

Safe to reopen workspaces? Deception stinks… yet, via TV, it's odourless.

Hey! Okay, ladies, okay, gents,
Go back to work, you malcontents
As pawns in your own government's
New viral risk experiments.

You've ministers. They make no scents.
They flash dumb numbers and percents
Till hopes decay by increments
To leave what life misrepresents.

We're fed false facts. Each voice invents
Its sins as if set in cements.
The lies lie clear though none repents.
Our fight-back's what this circumvents.

Here's where pure thoughtlessness ferments
And brews mere nods and blind assents.
So sense explodes. It's bomb fragments
On trains tight-packed, like mass events.

As war-dead, they'd be regiments.
With records, badges, documents,
Our lives allowed our loud laments.
It's peacetime, though, so truth torments.

MIXED MESSAGES

Shifty and shifting, government advice and policy became clear as mud... or quicksand.

They don't though they do, and they won't though they will
Soon stop or start testing the are or aren't ill.
They say down to me yet they say up to you.
We won't so we will, and we don't so we do.

Aware and alert to where viruses lurk.
We were staying home, now - knee-jerk - back to work.
Two metres apart till packed buses and trains.
We'll lose use of lungs by not using our brains.

It's all straightforward, in a roundabout way
When weighing which meaning they never quite say
While switching the weight of their words every day.
That's roundabout forward but not a straight say.

Like Nightingales opened so that they could close.
Like do and don't mask both your mouth and your nose.
Changes to changes to rules and to choices.
Lies, contradictions and misleading voices.

We've had quite enough of this duffness and guff
And blather and bluff and all similar stuff.
Grant us, we beg you, this opportunity…
Let us acquire whole heard immunity.

LANDSCAPES BY HIERONYMUS BOSCH

I wanted a poem like a painting of doomed universal suffering.

We're picturing scenes which this virus requires
Of tormented souls writhing in rolling shires
With agonies, corpses and funeral pyres
The whole of it floodlit by flames from those fires.

These sights are more hellish than Hogarth satires.
They've demons all dancing with dead priests and friars
On bodies of peasants and merchants and squires
While devils throw townsfolk from towers and spires.

Plague visions like these in which all life expires
As once declaimed by Mediaeval town criers
Seemed long-since abandoned to history's mires
But bounce back because we're led by fools and liars.

TELL JOHNSON AND TRUMP WE'RE NOT AT WAR

Both western leaders made speeches comparing battling the virus to past wars.

It has always seemed somewhat spurious
When wars end, that those deemed 'victorious'
Have labelled their mass deaths as glorious.

So, here's something even more curious…

No way is this pandemic war-ious,
Its lonely deaths slow and laborious.
Small wonder so many are furious.

War rhetoric's crass and injurious.

SHORT SENTENCES

Isolation eats into you.

Stuck in lockdown week on week.
It's no game, this hide-and-seek.
You soon sense you start to freak.
Don't we all? You're not unique.

Weather forecast stalls on bleak.
All the timbers start to creak.
Ship seems like it's sprung a leak.
Whole world's on a losing streak.

Pews unused in God's boutique.
Faith says turn the other cheek.
Some dumb stuff about the meek.
Virus decimates the weak.

Governed by this dodgy clique.
Info's double Dutch or Greek.
Can and can't work, meet or speak.
We do. Deaths rise. Second peak.

FIVE LINKED LIMERICKS

I started with one, but they kept coming. I like the different tone of each of these.

This virus for which there's no cure
Has sure made the world insecure.
In one killing bout
It's now taken out
A third of a million or more.

Me, though, I'm chilled to the marrow
That Britain's this lone wheelbarrow
Being pushed up Plague Road,
Our dead as its load,
By old boys from Eton and Harrow.

Global should be our polemic
To fight this fearful pandemic.
Yet Johnson's like Trump,
A go-alone gump,
Dumb, when we need academic.

Bad now but the next time far worse,
The virus, I mean, not my verse.
If you're infected
And it's detected
Sod limericks. Get to a nurse.

Corona has started to pack.
He's planning a break from this flak.
He's scribbled a note
And here's what he wrote:
'Stay safe, all. In Autumn I'm back.'

BECAUSE OF OUR IMPATIENCE

Scientists were saying that this pandemic would recur.

Covid returns by train again
By cruise ship and by plane again

We've outbreaks to contain again
As even more are slain again

Deaths enter that fast lane again
At speeds that are insane again

From Brisbane to Bahrain again
Ukraine to Bloemfontein again

In Britain and in Spain again
For Finn and Swede and Dane again

A U.S. hurricane again
As we see Trump abstain again

All contact to constrain again
Mass lockdowns to maintain again

And business down the drain again
And all that fear and pain again

Familiar refrain again
As ministers explain again

And go against the grain again
Their reasoning inane again

And when we all complain again
Excuses drop like rain again

More half-baked plans are lain again
While we fight back in vain again

Against the viral strain again
Which bounces back again, again…
again, again, again…

REOPENING SCHOOLS THE WEEK AFTER NEXT?

This was the government's first attempt to force schools to reopen.

Education, education, education.
It's a mantra that returns like constipation
And is greeted with bemused exasperation.
Our dictators issue it like rote dictation.
"Back to school, the first of June," their proclamation.

Education, education, education.
It's their lack of it that's causing consternation,
Their decision reached devoid of consultation.
Pack the playgrounds so our youngest generation
Can be rashly used to test viral gestation.

"Send 'em back! Send 'em back! Send 'em back!"
Fifty years ago, they used to chant that cack,
Only, then it was about repatriation.

Education, education, education.
Teach the virus to re-learn its germination.
Give it lessons in its own multiplication
From the classroom to the wider population
Spelling out the re-infection of our nation.

A WEEK OF GARDENING DURING LOCKDOWN

Much of the time, motivation wasn't easy.

Day one: you wonder whether to prune that rose.
Day two: you think of using the garden hose.
Day three: you're aghast just how fast the grass grows.
Day four: you'll mow the lawn soon, so you suppose.
Day five: your open gate really needs to close.
Day six: the sun shines and a gentle breeze blows.
Day seven: you sit out, doze, and the day just goes.

WHILE I'M OUT WALKING WITH MY BLOODY MUTT

Sometimes frustration's a bloke thing.

I'm out walking. I would be happy but
Nowhere's open. I do my bloody nut.

All the bloody pubs are still bloody shut
So's MacDonald's and bloody Pizza Hut.

I'm out walking. Down sunny streets I strut.
They're dead as hell. That gets my bloody gut.

Total dearth where I want a bloody glut.
Newsagents can't even sell bloody smut.

I'm out walking. Sport's off. I'm in a rut.
No goals, no runs, no pot or bloody putt.

The barber's closed, so no bloody haircut.
Gregg's shut. God! I want a bloody doughnut.

WISH LIST

Sometimes wishing helps to clarify the problems.

I wish we had a government which didn't cause offence.
I wish we had a government whose policies made sense.
I wish we had a government not prone to pure pretence.

I wish we had a government with leadership less dense.
I wish we had a government that read the evidence.
I wish we had a government worth pounds instead of
                                                          pence.

I wish we had a government wrought in the present tense.
I wish we had a government with more intelligence.
I wish we had a government not sold on self-defence.

I wish we had a government less fixed on the expense.
I wish we had a government whose care was more intense.
I wish we had a government whose lies were less
                                                          immense.

NORMAL

Fun poems are hard to find during a pandemic. Here's a lively one.

Normal? Take us back to that
Getting out of house or flat
Spending less time with the cat
Giving teachers back our brat.

Normal's without caveat
Open door and welcome mat
Meet the neighbour, stop and chat
Gossip, hearsay, chew the fat.

Normal's not some bureaucrat
It's just where we once were at
9 to 5 and all that tat
Mates who tell you you're a prat.

Normal's where I'd hang my hat
Pay my way and pay the VAT
Hairdresser and laundromat
Cafe, pub and cricket bat.

Normal's not this new format
Banged up like some caged lab rat
Spending night on night just sat
Trapped inside your habitat.

DOUBTERS' CREED

There are always those who care only for themselves.

We'll stick with herd immunity
And live in cattle-sheds.

We'll give up on community
And just take to our beds.

We'll break rules with impunity
And act like knuckleheads.

We'll fracture in disunity
And rip roadmaps to shreds.

We'll miss each opportunity
And turn down tests and meds.

We'll act with importunity
And dance while Covid spreads.

A POEM ABOUT YOU, DOMINIC CUMMINGS

As Johnson's unelected brain, Cummings devised Tory policy including lockdown, flagrantly broke his own rules, then lied his way out to remain in place as the slimeball covert power behind our lamentable government.

You set the rules for us to bear
But you don't toe that line.

For common people: common fare.
You self-indulgers dine,

Pick up a lie like an éclair,
Drink arrogance like wine.
.
You travel here, there, everywhere
As if your right's divine.

It's privilege, and you're the heir.
You're selfish by design.

You'd have us wash your underwear
When you should just resign.

You'd let us breathe infected air
So long as you were fine.

You're scum. You're numb cos all you care
About is thee and thine.

CAREHOME GHOSTS SPEAKING

As deaths in unprotected care homes with no PPE ran in ten of thousands, Matt Hancock simply lied that the government had protected them from the start of the pandemic.

Our problem was identified.
Their phones rang. Nobody replied.
Nothing we needed was supplied.

With figures altered, blame denied,
We were quietly pushed aside
By those on whom we'd all relied.

They didn't act. Meanwhile we died
Like flies sprayed by insecticide.
Where do their consciences reside?

Government's heartless underside:
'Our ring of care', they later lied
And claimed 'the science' was their guide.

PRESS CONFERENCE

*Disgraceful and deceptive interviews
became the government's norm.*

You mumble
And grumble

And bumble
And fumble

And jumble
And crumble

And stumble
And tumble.

Never humble, you.

We rumble you.

JOHNSON'S LATEST BABY

Newly a father, Johnson tried to quietly bin his other baby, the stillborn track'n'trace phone app which had been at the heart of his whole policy on the pandemic.

'World-beating!'
It's not a race.
Months too late
They've put in place
Test, track, trace.

Dodgy deal
On unsound base,
Cobbled at
A frantic pace,
Test, track, trace.

Far from what
We'll all embrace.
No time left,
Though, to replace
Test, track, trace.

System weak,
No style, no grace,
Fishy as
A plaice or dace,
Test, track, trace.

Distantly,
Not face-to-face,
Ill-equipped
For case-by-case
Test, track, trace.

Un-enforced,
Can't check or chase.
Isle-of-Wight
Proved far from ace.
Test, track, trace.

World-beating
Or world disgrace?
Baby-face
Gives a grimace.
Test, track, trace.

Will it work?
Just watch this space.
Chances are
We'll soon misplace
Test, track, trace.

ANTICIPATION

Just a joke about the distancing rule.

On the wall next to our side-door
Are two white boxes.

One contains our gas meter,
The other our electricity meter.

The two have been thus separated
since this house was built.

That was thirty years ago.
All that time, they've waited.

Now that the pandemic's arrived,
They're normalized.

They remain two meters apart,
Just as we now do.

WE

*Ongoing outrage that Cummings hadn't
gone, led to Johnson coming on TV to tell
us that we all needed to move on.*

We the people of this nation
We who've dealt with desperation
We who stuck in one location
We will not move on.

We who've gone through isolation
We hard-sold miscalculation
We deprived of preparation
We will not move on.

We short-changed with devastation
We hide-bound by legislation
We force-fed falsification
We will not move on.

We through hardship and privation
We who long for vaccination
We not prone to deviation
We will not move on.

We not fooled by fabrication
We not here for your dictation
We with higher expectation
We will not move on.

We withheld investigation
We with cause for consternation

We see through this situation
We will not move on.

We who've walked through death's damnation
We brim-full of accusation
We say with no hesitation
We will NOT move on.

POEM FOR MY PARTNER

Written for Gaynor after we'd had a rare row.

This lockdown life is losing sense.
As hidden price becomes expense
We think too much. These nights grow tense
And old disruptions recommence.

The simplest words can cause offence
And bring things to the boil, and hence
Like steam, emotions soon condense,
Turn sensitive to self-defence.

Our inner worlds now seem immense
While out beyond our garden fence
We see no trees. The wood's too dense
And pounds go while we count the pence.

Our love is real. The rest's pretence.
This poem's yours. It's frankincense.

TORY BASTARDS IN SEPTEMBER / OCTOBER

Stating the obvious, but it needed saying.

When their second peak comes, we know that they'll claim
Another hundred thousand, all of whom became
Dead were down to us lot. We screwed up their aim.

When their second peak comes, watch them rig the game.
They eased the lockdown, but they'll transfer the blame,
Tell us that it's our fault, set us centre-frame.

When their second peak comes, though they lit its flame
They'll claim exemption. They'll sell us the shame.
Who spread the virus? We're the ones they'll name.

ENDING THE HONEYMOON

Coming out of lockdown too soon, with its inevitable death-toll, was being pushed by every government spokesperson and many business leaders as if it would be in our interests.

Oh, pity this country which opens in June
And pity its people all out there too soon
Who mingle as if they were somehow immune.

The weather is lovely this hot afternoon
So who needs some poet to burst their balloon
With rhymes wrung like sad songs we croon out of tune?

But, just like those trees which bright blossoms festoon,
This virus now flowers, and our misfortune
Is that we're just leaving the last chance saloon.

IMAGINED GUEST

Lockdown made hospitality impossible.

Step in from the street that is virus-patrolled
We've warmth and a welcome behind this threshold
Away from precautions our leaders extolled
Come enter our humble home… lo & behold:

The walls… within which we do as we are told
The TV… which brings us the lies we are doled
Of care for the infirm, the ill and the old
And how the infection-rates will be controlled.

These rooms… a safe haven for our small household
Our garden… this rainbow, our small plot of gold
Where, although we sunbathe, we somehow stay cold
As if all those flowers were toadstools and mould.

Between floors and ceilings, here we're cubbyholed
Without tea or biscuits. Shop stocks have all sold.
We numb to this lifestyle in which we're enrolled
Designed to thwart dangers pandemics enfold.

SIGNING OUT

Another small tirade against the government's reckless retreat from lockdown.

Bloody bored by the blurred blather Boris bangs out,
Looks as if some zoo's let it's orang-outangs out.

Ending social distancing, a swan-song twangs out,
Ignoring wise warnings which 'the science' whangs out.

Weather's balmy, everybody barmy hangs out,
Deffo deaf to every death-knell that still clangs out.

They mill and mix and merge and, yeah, the whole
                                              gang's out,
Blank-blind to the Corona beast with its fangs out.

Within the week our lowered peak boomerangs… out.

SURROUNDED BY IDIOTS

The internet, social media, Trump etc. oozed conspiracy theories, fake solutions and denial.

Oh, for God's sake, give me a bloody break
From those who claim that this virus is fake,
Was made in a lab and freed by mistake,

Is just a mild cough and a slight headache
That's not passed on in a hug or handshake
And could be cured by potions you should take,

Or by powdered pangolin, bat or snake,
Gets killed by sun or a single snowflake,
Can be kept at bay by cheap charms they make,

Should be ignored with livelihoods at stake,
Means a mess of numbers much too opaque,
Boring, boring business. Why stay awake?

The pillars of wisdom shiver and shake.
Fools rule the earth. Feel it quiver and quake.

WE POETS, ADVERBALLY

*Sometimes writing turns into something
akin to a game.*

At first, we wondered why-erly
As symptoms showed perspire-ly,
But then deaths mounted spiral-ly.

Yet, poshly and esquire-ily,
Our government moved miry-ly
While acting guilt-denyer-ly.

We've bitten back require-ily,
Sarcastically and firy-ly,
With verses written viral-ly.

These came to us inspiral-ly
Each daily jotted diary-ly
On keyboard or else biro-ly.

Our leaders, unadmired-ly,
Colluded quite conspired-ly
Entirely pants-on-fired-ly.

To fiddled facts plain liar-ily
Evasively reply-ily,
While countless dropped haywire-ily.

Lungs labouring respire-ily,
Till legions more died dire-ily,
Precisely funeral pyre-ily.

IF I WERE THE VIRUS

*I like it when a poem seems to develop
its own storyline.*

If I were the virus
Sure, I'd participate
In crowded demos by
Those pro and anti hate.
They know they should distance
But they bite on my bait.

If I were the virus
I'd lend most of my weight
To disinformation
And its dumbed-down debate.
Why fuss with the facts when
You can just fabricate?

If I were the virus
I would willingly wait
To make Britain, Brazil
And America grate,
Each badly led state in
Such a badly led state.

If I were the virus
I'd do piracy, mate,
And come sailing straight home
With my contraband freight
Of smuggled infection
Which you'd all confiscate.

If I were the virus
I would bring you my plate
Of fresh flesh flash-fat-fried.
It's a dish I'd create.
Pal, I'd do death for you
And more, I'd be your fate.

GOVERNMENT WILL DUCK THE BLAME

More about our lame government planning to worm off the hook by passing on their burden of blame.

If there's a second surge as our lockdown's lifted
Watch the way the total blame's blatantly shifted.

They'll blame the people of this nation
For not liking isolation,
For our lack of separation,
For each too-close conversation,
For our crowds in shop, street, station,
For congested transportation,
For each march and demonstration.

When that surge puts more than before past surgery
Well, they'll quite simply purge themselves through
                                      perjury.

They'll blame the people of this nation
For our overpopulation,
For our poor cooperation,
For our too rash relaxation,
For our careless sanitation,
For kiss, hug and fornication,
For our in- and ex- halation.

We can't breathe.

FOR THOSE WHO STILL TRUST OUR GOVERNING GANG

Pre-Johnson, Theresa May's Tory government used the slogan 'strong & stable'. The last two lines are a nod to the Black Lives Matter protesters toppling the Bristol statue of slave-trader Edward Colston.

They were never strong and stable.
They were quick to drop that label.

Now, with Covid on the table,
They've proved neither wise nor able.

Tower of babble, not of Babel.
Silver-spooned from school to sable.

Let the vandals cut their cable.
History will fell their fable.

WHERE I WENT DURING LOCKDOWN

My friends know I'm forever making up rubbish jokes. Here's a poem based on some of them.

Went for a walk.
Met a friend.
We chatted:
Two meeters two metres apart.

Went shopping.
Asked for fisolate.
They had none.
Surely, they're supposed to sell fisolate.

Went to check progress.
They test too few of us.
They track a fraction of us.
They trace none of us.
We'll be lost without trace.

Went to make a coffee.
Used the teaspoon
For several hours.
I'm going stir-crazy.

Went to the bank
Wearing a mask and rubber gloves.
Last time I did that
I got a five-year stretch.

Went out on the street
8pm Thursdays
To clap for the NHS.
No problem.
The NHS knows how to treat clap.

Went to the pub
… only joking!

AS WE HIT MORE THAN SIXTY THOUSAND 'EXCESS' DEATHS

Written in a fit of righteous rage.

Finally, glaring governmental guilt
Wrings out its first few faltering admissions
That submissions of figures on fatalities got misread.

Mistakes were made, they said,
About the infection-rate and
Lockdown came too late and…

A slow trickle bled
Like a leaking tap
From the nothing which the Johnson junta said.

Some of their key advisors now agreed
That tens of thousands of UK deaths
Could have been so simply avoided.

These Gods have got round to revealing
What we mere mortals know they've been concealing
                                          for months.
Meanwhile, the vile fools who rule us remain in denial.

There should be a word in our language
For when plebs like us sit so sussed,
Sandwiched by killers, confessors and liars.

We need a word for when the street is wiser than the elite
Who steal our language from us, pickpocket education
                                                    from our kids,
Would persuade us that our black'n'white lives –
Leading to our blacker deaths - don't matter.

We must fight back, topple far more than 'precious'
                                                    statues,
Get their knees off our necks, breathe, reclaim literacy
From the stuttering gobshite gunfire of their Trumped-up
                                                    ignorance.

We will not be what they call us…
Their commies, cowards, commoners, coves,
Their pickaninnies, paupers, protesters, Pakis,
Their homeless, homos, migrants, mainliners, muggers,
Their anarchists, agitators, demonstrators, deviants,
Their terrorists, traitors, junkies, jailbirds, gypsies, Jews,
Their vandals, victims, losers, boozers, users,
Their loungers, liggers, scroungers, squatters, subversives,
Their infiltrators, immigrants, niggers, nihilists,
Their workforce, white trash and whatever…

We must kick back.
One word will do for us.
We'll reclaim a respectful name for ourselves.

LONER

*While some just got on with their days under
lockdown, others became almost as depressing
as the virus itself.*

No, my friend, I've never known a
Virus quite like this corona,
Killer that has no condoner,
Worse than curse of Judas, Jonah.

Some ignore it and have shown a
Blind eye turned to its persona.
Jobs done by each task-postponer.
Lawns mowed, cars washed by their owner.

Facetime, Skype, perhaps a phoner.
Every friend's become a moaner
Saying that they should have flown a
Way to stay in Barcelona.

TV platforms each brain-doner,
Street-shot stoner, Tory Sloaner.
Headcase lacking chaperoner,
Me, me, me, me monotoner.

Blown away by every groaner
Sounding like a gramophone or
Some such strictly selfish droner…
I could learn to be a loner.

WE'VE BEEN SHOPPED

More of my despair about our out-of-touch upper-class Tory politicians.

Take our lockdown back one week
Death toll could be half as bleak.
Not so, though, we're up shit-creek
Heading for our second peak.

In these times when truth can't speak
Disinherited, we meek
Must just wait for facts to leak.
They, meanwhile, play hide-and-seek.

We're stuck on this losing streak
Governed by the vain and weak
Each an in-bred posh pipsqueak,
All convinced that they're unique.

Hear their yachts begin to creak.
Smell their plots begin to reek.
See the cracks in their smug clique.
Trace the tracks their failures wreak.

Oh, but they play slim and sleek,
Glib of gob each gormless geek.
We should get mad. We should freak.
We should surely shout and shriek.

These cheap sales-staff think they're chic
Back in business. Quick sneak peek:
Figures which they twist and tweak
Flogging shit from their boutique.

SOME DAYS UNDER LOCKDOWN

Mental health became a growing concern.

Some days a lethargy settles like mist.
Sunrise gets cancelled. You hardly exist.
Time ties the hands of the watch on your wrist.

Some days thoughts clench as do teeth or a fist.
All the straight lines in your head seem to twist
Till you're your very own antagonist.

Some days come at you. And, God, they persist,
File all your faults and compile you their list.
Check it. They're dead right. There's nothing
                                          they've missed.

Open-heart work with no anaesthetist.
Some days you wish that some days would desist.
You fight through because you've learned to resist.

Some days it's simpler to simply get pissed.

EVENING WALK

Daily walks provided some semblance of respite.

Quietly ending a day that's been fine.
Quietly these streets assure me they're mine.

Quietly first through the woodland then park.
Quietly gardens preparing for dark.

Quietly insects inhabit the air.
Quietly governments pocket despair.

Quietly daily the patients all cough.
Quietly Covid still carries more off.

Quietly bodies are bagged up and gone.
Quietly moonlight moves in where sun shone.

THE VIRUS INVITES YOU…

As an end to lockdown loomed, many began to lower their guard.

The virus invites you…

… to throng through the crowds
cos they've opened the shops,

… to quit disinfecting
with wet-wipes and mops,

… to march in a demo
and fight with the cops,

… to dump your daft facemasks
and all such stage props,

… to mill round meat markets
and buy up the slops,

… to illegally rave
till the energy stops,

… to go with the good folk
whose guard slowly drops,

… to be in the fields
while it harvests fresh crops,

… to watch while the next wave
picks which lives it lops.

WE WEREN'T ALWAYS OLD

Because the virus predominantly attacked the elderly, the young were less afraid.

We used to feel safe back then when we were young
With the myriad myths to which we each clung.
It's thus we, along with those we were among,
Well knew that narcotics and bees never stung.

Though these were just stories which we were all strung,
We tackled that ladder and took every rung.
We blissfully danced to songs history sung
While blind to the blisters which hung from its tongue.

So, senselessly, we've somehow swayed on and swung
Unable to smell the dung our years have flung.
Yet, now in receipt of this crap we've been slung,
We're left with the wrinkles those decades have wrung.

We'd live with that legacy, bonus and bung,
But what's shot our story; what's suddenly sprung
Is luckless old age which has bowled in and brung
Its brutal new lodger to lurk in each lung.

THEIR NEW 'WORLD-CLASS' TRACK'N'TRACE PHONE APP

Faced with its utter failure, the Tories' flagship app was abandoned.

Now their app per-apps won't app-en.
Per-apps nobody's cl-app-en.
Per-apps they've been caught n-app-en.
Per-apps their app needs scr-app-en
Cos per-apps their app won't app-en.

True, their app per-apps won't app-en.
Per-apps some ch-app is fl-app-en.
Per-apps he'll get a sl-app-en.
Per-apps he need knee-c-app-en
Cos per-apps their app won't app-en.

Yeah, their app per-apps won't app-en.
Per-apps they've been cl-app-tr-app-en.
Per-apps their road m-app's cr-app 'n'
Per-apps its got a g-app in
Cos per-apps their app won't app-en.

JUST A LIST...

Lockdown life lacked a lot.

Just a list of what we've missed:

Restaurants and take-aways,
Holidays and hotel stays,

Telling jokes and hanging out,
Hearing what it's all about,

Meeting strangers, making friends,
All each chance encounter lends,

Coming home pissed as a rat,
Pals who drop in just to chat,

Diaries and making plans,
Airports, beaches, pools and tans,

Markets, malls and milling streets,
Matches won, even defeats,

All those jokes we've heard before,
Having fun, demanding more,

Celebrations, crowded rooms,
Foreign accents, strange perfumes,

Chatting while we stand in queues,
Not needing to watch the news,

Barbecues and pie'n'peas,
Lengthy drives and b'n'bs,

Festivals and busy bars
With live bands and loud guitars,

Time with those we love and know,
Days which don't end on a low,

Workplace, not computer screen,
Going where we've never been,

Life back as it was before,
All of this and much, much more.

RUN BY THE BULLINGDON BOYS

Our leaders persisted with their pretence that they were blameless.

Oh, doesn't our government just make you shiver?
They're on telly, gilding their lily that's liver,
Their garland of guilt. They admit not one sliver.
Whatever endeavour, they dither. We quiver.

Oh, doesn't their slithering just make you shiver?
They cleverly promise but never deliver,
Forever the taker though never the giver
While we and our assets get sold down the river.

LIFE WILL BE BETTER WHEN...

Optimism wasn't easy.

Butter becomes the one thing which we spread…
Viruses cease to be worthy of dread…

We are still here when such bastards have fled…
Medicine undermines murder's deathbed…

Innocent lives are not needlessly shed…
People not statues are our daily bread…

We've a clear view of what lies dead ahead…
Bullshit's removed from the paths that we tread…

No one needs food-banks cos everyone's fed…
We totally trust what our leaders have said…

Honesty's one thing to which we're all wed…
With language lain plain as light-beam or
                                        thread…

Trump's been defeated, is banged up or dead…
Truth isn't ticker-tape paper we shred…

… and so it goes on.

WHEN LIVES DON'T MATTER

There had been weeks of worldwide Black Lives Matter protests following the police killing of George Floyd.

There's never been a river that didn't have a source.
For sour white power there's Germanic, Viking, Norse.
Protesting and shouting, like corona, leaves you hoarse.
Terminating slavery takes more than Wilberforce.

Never was a marriage which is why there's no divorce.
Law stays as it was before and that's what they enforce.
Race is still being run and there's more trouble on the
                                                              course.
Wanna kill the rider? Maybe first you shoot the horse.

Deckchairs moved on sinking ships. Tap S.O.S. in Morse.
There's never been a murder which wasn't cruel and
                                                              coarse.
There again, the crime's the thing the courts'll all endorse.
They'll stain your streets with ketchup, the same old, same
                                                           old sauce.

TWO METRES DOWN TO ONE

Safer distancing was reduced to free up
flights, pubs, cafes, schools, hotels, etc.

By way of persistence
They've whittled resistance
From our coexistence.
Upon their insistence
We're halving the distance between us.

We'll risk our existence.
Is this tense? It *is* tense.
With brittle resistance,
Upon their insistence
We're halving the distance between us.

Stressed out by subsistence
In need of assistance
Left little resistance,
Upon their insistence
We're halving the distance between us.

IF THIS VIRUS KILLS ME, HERE'S WHAT I DID WELL

I allowed myself this personal poem.

Performing live at poetry gigs,
More than forty years not smoking cigs,

Saying unsayables wholly pissed,
Fifty years being an anarchist,

Never letting bastards grind me down,
Living mostly here in my hometown,

Visiting schools and inspiring kids,
Being a grandad to Jax and Syds,

Knowing merely people made these three:
Religion, cash, nationality,

Learning my lying harmed those I love,
Truth worn since like a PPE glove,

Married to Gaynor thirty-six years,
Mine's the luck, she's earned the claps and cheers,

Journalism; but, just as it looks:
The poor boil gruel while the rich cook books,

I've achieved little, changed none of that,
Showed off as a verbal acrobat,

As for the rest, got most of it wrong,
World out of tune while I sang along.

THE RAG TRADE REOPENS

Shops began to resume trading.

Lights have been switched on to banish the glooms
Surfaces polished and floors swept with brooms
Factories active, machinery vrooms.

Here we all are then. Now normal resumes.
Watch us emerging from our aching rooms
Ignoring warnings which dying exhumes.

Corona's still out there, and it assumes
Fabulous outfits, amazing costumes
In which to bury death's new brides and grooms.

Stepping out, we start inhaling those fumes
Strolling through gardens in which Covid blooms
To cinemas, churches, shops, pubs and tombs.

Weaving our futures on darkening looms
We are the fabric this virus consumes
The warp and weft of its business which booms.

We buy the clothing. The virus mushrooms.
Outfits for coffins, pandemic presumes.
Such putrid aromas! We purchase perfumes.

MAROONED

It seemed almost as if our politicians were on the side of the virus.

Left luckless through lockdown with no cloverleaf,
Now here we are, washed up on this sterile reef,
Thrown jabless and jobless in its sea of grief.

To lob us lies lightly's been their leitmotif,
The actual non-factual, beyond belief,
Since they said this virus would prove safe and brief.

It wasn't. It isn't. There's been no relief.
So many lives stolen, corona's the thief
They've aided, unarrested. This is our beef.

They're still bunched like grain-stalks in one lying sheaf,
Straws in the vain wind of their straw-headed chief,
Tongues at fresh tall-tales, today's aperitif.

WHY REOPEN EVERYTHING?

A tongue-in-cheek plea for longer lockdown.

Lonely proved tough until we found out how.
We've learned to love lockdown. Why end it now?
We get pissed at home. We don't miss the pub.
We've microwave meals. Sod take-away grub.

Why bring back barbers? We shave our own heads.
What's with getting up, when we've comfy beds?
Who needs offices? We work from our homes.
Restaurants are fit just for fat gastronomes.

Stuff waterparks, zoos and Alton Towers.
Cancel those day-trips. We'll stay at ours.
Holidays stress us. Staycations are best.
Have barbies. Hire hot tubs. Who needs the rest?

The kids have quit learning, given up school.
Swimming's for fishes. What good is a pool?
Why re-join gyms when we've set up our own.
Wide world's way outside our new comfort-zone.

We're stopping shopping jaunts. We buy on-line.
We're selling our cars. Don't need 'em. We're fine.
When milk gets delivered, why own a cow?
We love you, lockdown. Don't quit on us now.

WHEN THIS VIRUS HITS ITS SECOND SPIKE

A threnody is a death song. To thresh means both to thrash (as in terminal viral convulsions) and to violently rip apart what's been reaped (usually grain, but here humans).

Yeah, you will be the death of us
The dose of crystal meth of us
That steals the very breath of us.

You'll be the no, not yes of us
That's not what we would guess of us
But leads to loads more less of us.

You'll crash the cash and creche of us
And lash us to the mesh of us
Flash-fry and flay the flesh of us.

You'll Manson the address of us.
Throughout this final sesh of us
You'll cherish your mad mess of us.

You'll relish the distress of us.
Force fetid from the fresh of us
And threnody from thresh of us.

SEA FEVER

by John Masefield

The original version.

I must go down to the seas again, to the lonely sea and the sky,
And all I ask is a tall ship and a star to steer her by,
And the wheel's kick and the wind's song and the white sail's shaking,
And a grey mist on the sea's face, and a grey dawn breaking.

I must go down to the seas again, for the call of the running tide
Is a wild call and a clear call that may not be denied;
And all I ask is a windy day with the white clouds flying,
And the flung spray and the blown spume, and the sea gulls crying.

I must go down to the seas again, to the vagrant gypsy life,
To the gull's way and the whale's way where the wind's like a whetted knife;
And all I ask is a merry yarn from a laughing fellow-rover,
And quiet sleep and a sweet dream when the long trick's over.

SEA FEVER

by Nick Toczek

My fairly faithful re-working for those who packed beaches as soon as we got hot weather.

We must go down the seafront again, to the crowded
                                       beach and we'll lie,
And we'll all bask with a death wish and folly to steer us
                                                                by,
And to feel sick and the cough's song and the quite pale
                                                   shaking,
And a great risk to the whole race, and the next wave
                                                 breaking.

We must go down to that beach again, though the call for
                                                 such suicide
Is a rash call and a massed call with common sense defied;
But we'll all bask on a sunny day with virus clouds flying,
And the young prey, and the grown doomed, and the
                                                 wardfuls dying.

We must go down with disease again, and a flagrant loss
                                                 of life,
While the ghouls sway, and the wraiths sway where the
                                                 plague's like sweated strife;
And all we ask is a miracle from Allah or Jehovah,
Or a quiet step to sweet death when the Covid's over.

COVID-19'S LEICESTER PRESS CONFERENCE

An alarming local spike led to Leicester
going straight back into full lockdown.

Let's meet human life's digester
Mankind's merciless molester
Homo sapiens detester
Local lung-function divester

Keen on beach bum and protester
Fan of party and fiesta
And of every dumb investor
In some won't-stay-safe siesta.

He's dropped in, this mirthless jester,
Just to force the mass to fester.
His rehearsal's here to test a
Second spike's autumn semester.

We were best but face our bester
Whose mere presence must suggest a
New peak pestilence to pester
This poor populace of Leicester.

BUILD BUILD BUILD

*Johnson adopted this slogan to launch his
'New Deal' scheme to reconstruct Britain.*

While Leicester's under lockdown
All the rest of us pretend
That now we need to knock down
What we've got and strife will end.

The virus is returning,
The economy is shite,
So let's just turn the nation
Into one big building site.

We queue outside our food banks
While our jobs are on the line.
Cue the diggers, bricks and planks.
Hey presto! We'll be fine.

Dreadful March, April and May
Catastrophic June.
Build, build, build. Bulldoze away
Cos the pubs reopen soon.

Companies are going bust.
This pandemic's at its height.
Bexit turns our trade to dust.
Bob the Builder puts it right.

A CORONAVIRUS TIMELINE

December 2019

31st: China warns World Health Organisation (WHO) of new virus.

January 2020

23rd: Wuhan goes into lockdown.

24th: Article in UK medical journal, The Lancet, warns of acute danger to human life from virus. Prime Minister Boris Johnson misses first COBRA (Cabinet Office Briefing Rooms) meeting re virus.

29th: Johnson misses second COBRA meeting re virus.

30th: World Health Organisation (WHO) declares international public health emergency.

31st: Two people in UK test positive for virus. National Health Service (NHS) England declares first ever level four critical incident. Government declines invitation to join Europe scheme to source personal protective equipment (PPE).

February 2020

5th: Johnson misses third COBRA meeting re virus.

12th: Exeter University study warns that, if unchallenged, virus could infect 45m people in UK. Johnson misses fourth COBRA meeting re virus.

14th: Johnson starts 'working holiday' at Chevney. Brief summaries of issues are accepted. Anything longer rejected by Johnson's chief aide, Dominic Cummings. Johnson focuses on securing divorce so he can announce his engagement to his pregnant girlfriend.

15th: Johnson misses fifth COBRA meeting re virus.

26th: Half a million Britons could die according to a leaked UK government worst case scenario document.

27th: First confirmed case in Northern Ireland.

28th: Confirmation of the first British death from Coronavirus (a man quarantined aboard the Diamond Princess cruise ship in Japan).

29th: NHS bosses warn of PPE shortages & a nightmare facing

health service. Johnson goes to Checkers & announces engagement & pregnancy.

March 2020

2nd: Johnson attends sixth COBRA meeting re virus.

3rd: Scientists urge government to advise the public not to shake hands. Johnson boasts on national TV of having visited hospital with infected patients & shaken hands 'with everybody, you'll be pleased to know'.

5th: Johnson says 'as far as possible it should be business as usual'. Greece closes all schools, as Iran & Italy have already done. First coronavirus death in UK where confirmed cases pass 100. Flybe goes into administration.

6th: Johnson announces £46 million to fund research into vaccine & rapid diagnostic testing then shakes hands with scientists working on antibody test.

7th: UK cases pass 200. Johnson joins 82,000 closely-packed spectators at 6-Nations rugby match.

9th: France bans large events & introduces stricter distancing. Ireland cancels St Patrick's Day parades. UK government says there's 'no rationale' for cancelling sporting events.

10th: 4-day Cheltenham Horseracing Festival begins, 250,000 people attend. UK health minister, Nadine Dorries, tests positive for virus.

11th: The WHO declares global pandemic. Madrid, epicentre of Spain's virus crisis, closes all schools. 3,000 Atletico Madrid fans attend match in Liverpool.

12th: While Germany & South Korea lead world in mass testing & contact tracing, UK government abandons it in favour of 'herd immunity', a strategy projected to kill 250,000 UK citizens. Chief medical officers raise UK risk level from moderate to high. Johnson announces 'We are not, repeat, not closing schools now'. First virus death in Wales.

13th: First virus death in Scotland. 2019-2020 football Premier League season suspended. BBC Radio 1 cancels Big Weekend music festival.

14th: Confirmed cases in UK pass 1,000. France closes schools & universities. Ireland shuts all educational institutions. Germany closes schools, nurseries & universities. The WHO declares Europe epicentre of global pandemic. UK government persists with 'herd immunity', aiming to infect over 60% of Britons. Johnson lifts restrictions on arrivals in the UK of people from known virus hotspots, including Wuhan, Italy & Iran. UK government advises NHS staff to wear less PPE in all but high risk situations. First of two Cardiff Arena concerts by The Stereophonics. Panic buying in shops & supermarkets of pasta, hand gels, toilet paper, etc.

15th: Germany tightens border restrictions. Ireland closes pubs. Second Stereophonics Cardiff Arena gig (15,000 attend over 2 nights).

16th: Imperial College study concludes that half a million Britons could die. Johnson advises against 'non-essential travel' & asks people not to go to pubs. UK government begins daily 5pm televised press conferences. UK deaths reach 55 as cases pass 1,500. Government calls for UK companies to manufacture ventilators, Johnson joking that this should be called 'Operation Last Gasp'.

17th: France goes into lockdown. Chancellor, Rishi Sunak, announces £330bn loan guarantees for UK businesses. Foreign office advises against non-essential foreign travel. UK cinema chains close.

18th: WHO says contact tracing must be 'backbone of every country's response to the virus'. UK virus deaths pass 100. Government announces all schools to close on 20th (except for children of key workers & vulnerable children). Glastonbury Festival cancelled.

19th: As 'a stiff broom' to free up beds, government tells NHS hospitals to move all elderly patients into care homes, even those with the virus. In all, more than 4,000 are moved. First virus death in Northern Ireland.

20th: UK finally closes schools & pubs. Government wrongly claims PPE shortages have been completely resolved. Johnson announces he's hoping to see his mother on Mothers' Day. Sunak announces government will pay 80% of wages of employees not working. Johnson closes all cafes, pubs and restaurants.

22nd: Johnson asks people not to visit their mothers on Mothers' Day.

23rd: Johnson finally announces UK-wide partial lockdown.

24th: Health Secretary, Matt Hancock, announces plan to build temporary NHS Nightingale Hospital in London. Scottish parliament closes. Church of England closes all buildings.

25th: Prince Charles tests positive for coronavirus. UK parliament shuts down. Death of first two working NHS doctors.

26th: First national weekly Thursday evening 'Clap for Carers' tribute.

27th: Johnson & Hancock test positive for virus. Both self-isolate, as does Chief Medical Adviser Chris Whitty after showing symptoms. Cummings breaks lockdown rules (devised by him) by driving 250 miles to Durham with wife & child.

29th: First virus death of NHS nurse.

30th: Cummings self-isolates after claiming to have been showing symptoms.

April 2020

2nd: Matt Hancock ends self-isolation & promises 100,000 daily tests by end of April. Care homes are told that 'negative tests are not required prior to transfer of patients into care homes' - i.e. Covid-infected elderly should be moved too.

3rd: NHS Nightingale Hospital London opens.

5th: Johnson hospitalised as symptoms worsen. Scotland's Chief Medical Officer, Catherine Calderwood, resigns after breaking lockdown by twice visiting her second home.

9th: Johnson moved into intensive care.

11th: Growing complaints from NHS workers about insufficient PPE.

12th: 'Official' UK death toll reaches 10,000. Johnson discharged from hospital. Cummings drives wife (on her birthday) & son from Durham to Barnard Castle & back (60-mile round trip).

15th: Cummings drives family 250 miles back to London. Testing in care homes begins with the introduction - far too late - of 'a policy of testing' all residents prior to admission.

18th: Government admits PPE is running out but says 400,000 PPE gowns will tomorrow arrive from Turkey.

19th: PPE from Turkey fails to arrive.

21st: Government ignored PPE being made in UK so, despite shortage, millions of these items were shipped from UK to Europe. Frontline health worker deaths reach 80. Hancock says government is 'throwing everything' a developing vaccine & announces £42.5m for clinical trials at Imperial College London & Oxford University.

22nd: Government u-turn on testing which they ended six weeks ago but now adopt. Turkish PPE shipment, from a t-shirt maker, arrives in the UK.

23rd: First human coronavirus vaccine tests in Europe begin at Oxford University.

25th: Official UK death toll passes 20,000. True total more like 40,000.

28th: Office for National Statistics (ONS) reports that a third of virus deaths in England & Wales are in care homes.

30th: Johnson claims his government has 'succeeded in avoiding the tragedy that engulfed other parts of the world'. In fact Britain's death toll is the third highest in the world.

May 2020

5th: Official UK deaths near 30,000 while report in The Times gives real figure at about 55,000, the highest in Europe. Trials of government's overdue & much hyped (Johnson called it 'world beating') contact tracing app start on the Isle of Wight. Virgin Atlantic to shed 3,000 jobs & end operations at Gatwick Airport due to pandemic. Professor Neil Ferguson, whose advice triggered lockdown, resigns from the Scientific Advisory Group for Emergencies (SAGE) after his 'married lover' broke lockdown rules by visiting his home.

7th: Government's entire Turkish shipment of PPE proves substandard & unusable.

10th: Government slogan 'stay at home, protect the NHS, save lives' is changed to the vaguer 'stay alert, control the virus, save lives'. In a 7pm TV address to the nation Johnson announces a phased end to lockdown, beginning next day with construction workers & those in manufacturing returning to work. Passengers entering UK on international flights (except from Ireland) to quarantine for two weeks.

11th Government publishes 50-page document detailing the phased ending of lockdown. Air passengers from France exempted from quarantine. Teaching unions describe government plans to reopen schools on 1 June as reckless & unsafe. UK Statistics Authority rebukes Hancock for manipulating testing figures.

12th: ONS statistics: UK virus deaths exceed 40,000 and include over 11,000 care home deaths. Sunak extends government funding of furlough scheme until October.

17th: Business secretary Alok Dharma announces a further £84m to help mass produce vaccine being developed at Oxford University.

18th: Garden centres, sports courts & recycling centres reopen. Loss of smell & taste added as virus symptoms. Hancock claims 21,000 contact tracers have been recruited.

19th: Major security issues identified in the government's tracing app being tested on the Isle of Wight.

20th: Johnson states track and trace system will be in place by 1 June. Rolls Royce to cut 9,000 jobs due to pandemic. Those hospitalised falls below 10,000 for first time since March.

21st: NHS Confederation warns time is running out to finalise a test, track & trace strategy to avoid a second surge in cases.

22nd: SAGE publishes report claiming low risk from reopening schools on 1 June.

23rd: Scandal of Cummings breaking lockdown dominates UK news for next few days.

28th: NHS Test & Trace is launched. Durham police to press no charges over Cummings' 'minor breach' of lockdown rules. EasyJet to cut 4,500 jobs due to pandemic. Tenth (and final) weekly clap for carers.

29th: Sunak announces Coronavirus job retention scheme and payments to self-employed will all end in October. President Donald Trump announces U.S. to sever all ties with WHO.

30th: Some government scientific advisers criticise lifting lockdown while cases & deaths are still high. Johnson relaxes restrictions on 2.2m vulnerable people who've been 'shielding' at home.

June 2020

1st: Without parliamentary scrutiny, as has become their practice, Johnson's government again relax lockdown by opening car & caravan showrooms, outdoor sports amenities & outdoor non-food markets. Six people can gather outdoors. Primary schools reopen. Horse racing & snooker recommence.

2nd: Virus deaths lowest since March. Hancock further rebuked by

UK Statistics Authority for using vastly exaggerated figures on testing. Government ends daily televised briefings.

5th: UK 'official' death toll passes 40,000. British Medical Association (BMA) calls for further use of face coverings.

6th: Black Lives Matter demonstrations draw vast crowds across UK (& globally). These continue throughout June.

7th: Government scientific advisor Professor John Edmunds says delayed lockdown 'cost a lot of lives'. Hancock reponds by claiming government 'took the right decision at the right time'.

8th: 14-day quarantine for all new UK arrivals, including returning holidaymakers. BP to shed 10,000 jobs due to pandemic.

9th: Government abandons plans for all primary pupils to resume schooling before end of summer term. Black, Asian & minority ethnic (BAME) people found to be twice as likely to die from virus. Quarter of UK workforce (8.9m) being paid by government at cost to date of £19.6bn.

10th: Professor Neil Ferguson says if lockdown had begun one week earlier, UK deaths could have been halved.

12th: ONS says UK economy shrank by 20.4% in April, largest monthly reduction ever.

13th: Members of two families can now stay together overnight in what government calls 'support bubble'.

15th: Face covering becomes mandatory on public transport. Non-essential shops reopen. Zoos & safari parks reopen. Places of worship reopen for private prayer. Some secondary pupils return to school.

16th: Dexamethasone found to reduce coronavirus deaths.

17th: Premier League football resumes.

18th: Government abandons its contact tracing app. AstraZeneca & Oxford University reach deal to manufacture & stockpile potential vaccine.

19th: UK's Covid-19 alert level lowered from 4 (severe risk, high transmission) to 3 (substantial risk, general circulation).

23rd: Johnson announces that from 4 July, social distancing to halve to 1 metre to coincide with reopening of pubs, restaurants, hotels & hairdressers.

24th: Imperial College London begins human trials of its vaccine. BMA warns of 'real risk' of second wave of coronavirus.

25th: Heatwave sees crowded beaches, parks, etc

26th: Intu Properties, owners of many large UK shopping centres, goes into administration due to pandemic.

29th: Leicester goes back into lockdown after spike in coronavirus cases.

ABOUT NICK TOCZEK

Photo by John Bolloten

Nick Toczek is a British writer and performer who lives in his hometown of Bradford in Yorkshire. He's published more than fifty books, released numerous albums (of music and of spoken word) and has visited dozens of countries as a writer in schools. He's also a professional magician, puppeteer, radio presenter and music journalist.

RECENT PUBLICATIONS

Voices In My Head (Caboodle Books, 2020) - book of poetry.

Dragons Are Back! (Caboodle Books, 2016) - book of dragon poems for children.

Haters, Baiters And Would-Be Dictators (Routledge, 2016) - book on history of anti-Semitism.

Cats'n'Bats'n'Slugs'n'Bugs (Caboodle Books, 2009) - book of children's poems about creatures.

Number, Number, Cut A Cucumber (Caboodle Books, 2009) - book of poems for younger children.

Me And My Poems (Caboodle Books, 2008) - poems for children.

ALBUM RELEASES

Nick Toczek has also collaborated on a number of releases of his poetry and lyrics with musical backing, including:

Nick Toczek & Signia Alpha

Shooting The Messenger (Mutiny 2000 Records, 2020) on vinyl LP, CD & download.

> 'The laid-back, funky, jazz rock vibe that characterises most of this album complements Toczek's distinctive and, as ever, reassuringly calm, but equally commanding Yorkshire burr perfectly.'
> Vive Le Rock!   (Mar/Apr 2020)

Nick Toczek & Thies Marsen

The Bavariations Album (Not-A-Rioty Records, 2019) - on CD & download.

Death And Other Destinations: The Second Bavariations Album (Not-A-Rioty Records, 2020) - on vinyl LP & download.

> 'Setting poems against music is hazardous. Nick Toczek is, thankfully, the kind of poet whose lifestyle and experience aptly suit him to the process. … His counterpart is, suitably, a Bavarian punk and indie musician who … has produced this stunning, innovative album.'
> RnR Magazine (2019)

All the above are available via Nick's website (see below).

CONTACT DETAILS, WEBSITES & INFO.

Nick's website: www.nicktoczek.com
Schools bookings via: www.authorsabroad.com
Wikipedia pages: en.wikipedia.org/wiki/Nick_Toczek
Nick's email: nick.toczek@gmail.com

Also available from Mutiny 2000 Publications

Bradford's Noise Of The Valleys
by Gary Cavanagh and Matt Webster

Bradford's Noise Of The Valleys is a series of books and CDs that tell the story of the music scene of Bradford and the surrounding areas, including Keighley and Halifax, from the 1960s onwards. **Volume One** covers the years 1967 to 1987, **Volume 2** continues the history between 1988 and 1998.

The books contain hundreds of 'rock family trees' and feature individual profiles of bands and artists and many local clubs and venues. The pages are packed with contemorary photos, articles, posters and images. These cover a massive range of musical styles from pop and rock to folk and blues to indie and punk to hardcore and doom metal to the dance scene.

Also available to compliment the books is a range of CDs showcasing many of the featured bands, including; Tasmin Archer, Terrorvision, New Model Army, Kiki Dee, Paradise Lost, 1919, Verity, The Accent, Smokie, Zed, Slammer, Skeletal Family, Psycho Surgeons, The Invaders, The Negatives, Embrace, Western Dance, Pianoman and Nick Toczek.

'...this work of breathtaking scholarship. Books like this send you spiralling back through the landscapes of your memory...' Ian Clayton

bradfordnoise.com

www.ingramcontent.com/pod-product-compliance
Lightning Source LLC
Chambersburg PA
CBHW030040100526
44590CB00011B/274